MEN OF FAITH

John
Hyde

Francis McGaw

BETHANY HOUSE PUBLISHERS
MINNEAPOLIS, MINNESOTA 55438
A Division of Bethany Fellowship, Inc.

Formerly entitled *Praying Hyde*.

John Hyde
Francis McGaw

Library of Congress Catalog Card Number 86-70907

ISBN 0-87123-909-4

Copyright © 1970
Bethany Fellowship, Inc.
All Rights Reserved

Published by Bethany House Publishers
A Division of Bethany Fellowship, Inc.
6820 Auto Club Road, Minneapolis, Minnesota 55438

Printed in the United States of America

WOMEN OF FAITH SERIES

Amy Carmichael
Corrie ten Boom
Florence Nightingale
Gladys Aylward
Hannah Whitall Smith
Isobel Kuhn
Mary Slessor
Joni

MEN OF FAITH SERIES

Borden of Yale
Brother Andrew
C. S. Lewis
Charles Finney
Charles Spurgeon
Eric Liddell
George Muller
Hudson Taylor
Jim Elliot
Jonathan Goforth
John Hyde
John Wesley
Martin Luther
Samuel Morris
Terry Waite
William Carey
William Booth
D. L. Moody

John and Betty Stam

I have fought the good fight, I have finished the course, I have kept the faith; henceforth there is laid up for me a crown of righteousness, which the Lord, the righteous judge, shall give to me at that day; and not to me only, but unto all them also that love his appearing. —II Timothy 4:7-8

PREFACE

Sometimes we speak of prayer as a privilege. Other times we may speak of it as a responsibility. In John Hyde's life the need of prayer and the privilege of prayer came together as one.

John Hyde set God's name apart by prayer. The Lord transformed his life; He led him to share His intercessions, and His sufferings, as well as His joys.

God's work on the earth was not an issue of fatalism in John Hyde's theology. He knew that men could share the authority of God and release the work of God in the lives of those who need salvation and deliverance. Through intercessory prayer Mr. Hyde was able to make a highway for God to work in conventions, churches, and in personal lives.

He proved that prayer was an evangelical force in India when, by faith, he claimed one soul a day, then two, then four. Those prayers were answered as he went out among the people and witnessed for Christ. He was a co-worker with Christ.

We all recognize that God uses His servants for different purposes. Luther carried the message of justification by faith. Wesley heralded the grace of sanctification. Hudson Taylor encouraged thousands to spread the gospel by faith in God's provision. John Hyde explored new territory in the vast ministry of prayer. I think we are safe in saying that John Hyde was an apostle of prayer.

In the light of this unusual testimony two things should be kept in mind. First, God is original in each of our redeemed personalities. The Apostle Paul said, "There are *diversities of operations,* but it is the *same God* which worketh all in all." God will not give everyone the same ministry John Hyde had.

Second, if the Holy Spirit controls our lives He will lead us into an effective life of prayer—not a copy of John Hyde's, but a distinctive prayer life of our own. He teaches us all to pray.

I don't know how this book will affect you. It made me realize there was much spiritual ground to be possessed. We can only ask God that we might learn to know the voice of the Holy Spirit that calls us to pray.

H. J. Brokke

PRAYING HYDE

Christ in the Home

JOHN HYDE, The Apostle of Prayer, as he was often called, was reared in a home where Jesus was an abiding guest, and where the family in that home breathed an atmosphere of prayer.

I was well acquainted with John's father, Smith Harris Hyde, D.D., during the seventeen years he was pastor of the Presbyterian Church at Carthage, Illinois. Dr. Herrick Johnson, of Chicago, shortly before he died wrote these words:

> Hyde's father was of rare proportion and balance, a healthful soul, genial and virile, firm of conviction, of good scholarly attainment, of abundant cheer and bent on doing for God to the best of his ability.

Personally I knew Dr. Hyde to be a courteous, loving husband. I knew him to be a firm yet sympathetic father. I knew the sweet-spirited, gentle, music-loving, Christ-like Mrs. Hyde. I knew each one of the three boys and three girls who grew up in the home.

Often I have eaten at their table. Twice I have been with the family when crepe was on the door; once when Mrs. Hyde was taken away, and again when dear John's body was brought home and lovingly laid to rest in Moss Ridge Cemetery. Often I have kneeled with them and have, as a young minister, been strangely moved when dear Dr. Hyde poured out his heart to God as he prayed at the family altar. I knew him in his church and in the Presby-terial meetings. He was a noble man of God.

Under God, his congregation was built up, and he was a leader among his minis-terial brethren. I have frequently heard Dr. Hyde pray the Lord of the harvest to thrust out laborers into His harvest. He would pray this prayer both at the family altar and from his pulpit. It is, therefore, no strange thing that God called two of his sons into the Gospel ministry, and one of his daughters, for a time, into active Chris-tian work.

A minister once said in my hearing, "My son will never follow me into the ministry. He knows too well the treatment a minister receives at the hands of the people."

Dr. Hyde magnified his office and rejoiced to give his sons up to a life of hardship and trial.

Why are there thousands of churches in our country without pastors today? Why are millions in the foreign field yet waiting for the human voice to proclaim to them the everlasting Gospel of the Son of God?

Today I read the statement by a former missionary in India, Dr. W. B. Anderson, that a hundred million people in India today have not heard of Jesus Christ, and as things are now have not the remotest chance to hear about him. There are other millions in Africa and other countries in the same Christless ignorance. Why is it so? Because prayer closets are deserted, family altars are broken down, and pulpit prayers are formal and dead!

John Hyde was an answer to prayer, and when in other years he prayed in India, God raised up scores of native workers in answer to his prayers. The Great Head of

the Church has provided one method for
securing laborers. Prayer!

Holy Ground

In the Tabernacle of Moses there was
one room so sacred that only one man of
all the thousands of Israel was ever permitted to enter it; and he on one day only
of all the three hundred and sixty-five days
of the year. That room was the Holy of
Holies.

The place where John Hyde met God
was holy ground. The scenes of his life are
too sacred for common eyes. I shrink from
placing them before the public.

But near the prayer closet of John Hyde
we are permitted to hear the sighing and
the groaning, and to see the tears coursing
down his dear face, to see his frame weak-
ened by foodless days and sleepless nights,
shaken with sobs as he pleads, "O God,
give me souls or I die!"

Decision

His decision to go to the foreign field
came about in this way: His oldest brother,

Edmund, was in seminary preparing to preach, and was also a Student Volunteer for the foreign field. During one summer vacation Edmund was engaged in Sunday school mission work in Montana. He contracted the mountain fever. The doctor advised his speedy return to his home in Illinois; so with his railroad ticket and instructions to the different conductors pinned to the lapel of his coat, he started. He became delirious before reaching home, but arrived safely. After a few days he passed away.

John, who was already expecting to preach, was deeply impressed by his brother's death. There would be a break in the ranks on the foreign field, and he wondered if it were not God's will for him to step into the gap.

The decision was not reached till the next year, his last in seminary. Late one Saturday night he went to a classmate's room and asked him for all the arguments he could furnish on the question of the foreign field. His classmate told him that it was not argument he needed; what he should do was to go to his room, get on his knees before God, and stay there till the question was settled. The next morning at Chapel he told his friend that it was settled, and his shining face was enough to show which way the decision had been made.

Sailing Day and the Voyage

The mighty deep, the great rolling waves, the days on days of water, water, only water, the feet lifted up from the dear homeland and not yet planted on the new homeland—all these furnish suggestion and opportunity for thoughtful meditation.

To John Hyde this voyage in the autumn of 1892 was a time of heart-searching and prayer. He had received a letter to which he afterwards made reference in an Indian publication:

> My father had a friend who greatly desired to be a foreign missionary, but was not permitted to go. This man wrote me a letter directed in care of the ship. I received it a few hours out of New York harbor. He urged me to seek for the baptism of the Holy Spirit as the great qualification for mission work. When I had read the letter I crumpled it up in anger and threw it on the deck.

Did this friend think that I had not received the baptism of the Spirit, or that I would think of going to India without this equipment? I was angry. But by and by better judgment prevailed and I picked up the letter and read it again. Possibly I did need something which I had not yet received. The result was that during the rest of that voyage I gave myself much to prayer that I might indeed be filled with the Spirit and know by an actual experience what Jesus meant when he said: Ye shall receive power, when the Holy Ghost is come upon you: and ye shall be My witnesses both in Jerusalem, and in all Judea and Samaria, and unto the uttermost part of the earth.

These prayers on shipboard were finally answered in a marvelous way.

First Years in India

At first John Hyde was not a remarkable missionary. He was slow of speech. When a question or remark was directed to him he seemed not to hear, or if he heard, he seemed a long time in framing a reply. His hearing was slightly defective and this, it was feared, would hinder him in acquiring the language. His disposition was gentle and quiet, he seemed to be lacking in the enthusiasm and zeal which a young missionary should have. He had a wonderful pair of blue eyes. They seemed to search into the very depth of your inmost being, and they seemed also to shine out of the soul of a prophet.

On arriving in India, he was assigned the usual language study. At first he went to work on this, but later neglected it for Bible study. He was reprimanded by the committee, but he replied: "First things first."

He argued that he had come to India to teach the Bible, and he needed to know it before he could teach it. And God by His Spirit wonderfully opened up the Scriptures to him. Nor did he neglect language study. He became a correct and easy speaker in Urdu, Punjabi, and English; but away and above that, he learned the language of heaven, and he so learned to speak that he held audiences of hundreds of Indians spellbound while he opened to them the truths of God's Word.

The Punjab Prayer-Union

In every revival there is a divine side and a human side. In the Welsh revival the divine element comes out prominently. Evan Roberts, the leader under God, seems in a sense to have been a passive agent, mightily moved upon in the night seasons by the Holy Spirit. There was no organization and very little preaching—comparatively little of the human element. The Sialkot revival which is now to be described, while just as certainly sent down from heaven, seems not so spontaneous. There was under God, organization; there was a certain amount of definite planning, and there were seasons of long continued prayer.

Preceding the revival was the organization of the Punjab Prayer-Union.

The principles of this union are stated in the form of questions which were signed by those becoming members.

Are you praying for quickening in your own life, in the life of your fellow-workers, and in the Church?

Are you longing for greater power of the Holy Spirit in your own life and work, and are you convinced that you cannot go on without this power?

Will you pray that you may not be ashamed of Jesus?

Do you believe that prayer is the great means for securing this spiritual awakening?

Will you set apart one-half hour each day as soon after noon as possible to pray for this awakening, and are you willing to pray till the awakening comes?

John Hyde was associated with this prayer union from its beginning. The members of the prayer union lifted up their eyes according to Christ's command and saw the fields, white to the harvest. In the Book they read the immutable promises of God. They saw the one method of obtaining this spiritual awakening, even by prayer. They set themselves deliberately, definitely, and desperately to use the means till they secured the result.

The Sialkot revival was not an accident nor an unsought breeze from heaven. Charles G. Finney says:

A revival is no more a miracle than a crop of wheat. In any community revival can be secured from heaven when heroic souls enter the conflict determined to win or die—or if need be to win and die!—The kingdom of heaven suffereth violence, and the violent take it by force.

The First Sialkot Convention

Jesus had many unnamed disciples. He had the Twelve, but in the inner circle nearest to Himself were the special three: Peter, James and John. Hundreds came to Sialkot and helped mightily by prayer and praise. But God honored a few men as leaders. He laid a great burden of prayer upon the hearts of John N. Hyde, R. McChenye Paterson, and George Turner for this wonderful convention.

There was need for a yearly meeting for Bible study and prayer, where the spiritual life of the workers, pastors, teachers, and evangelists, both foreign and native, could be deepened. The church-life in the Punjab (as indeed in all India) was far below the Bible standard; the Holy Spirit was so little honored in these ministries that few were being saved from among the Christless millions. Sialkot was the place selected for this meeting.

Before one of the first conventions Hyde and Paterson waited and tarried one whole month before the opening day. For thirty days and thirty nights these godly men waited before God in prayer. Do we wonder that there was power in the convention? Turner joined them after nine days.

For twenty-one days and twenty-one nights these three men prayed and praised God for a mighty outpouring of His power! Three human hearts that beat as one, yearning, pleading, crying, and agonizing over the church of India and the myriads of lost souls. Three renewed human wills that by faith linked themselves as with hooks of steel to the omnipotent will of God. Three pairs of fire-touched lips that out of believing hearts shouted, "It shall be done!"

Do you who read these words look at those long-continued vigils, those days of fasting and prayer, those nights of wakeful watching and intercessions, and do you say: "What a price to pay!" Then I point you to scores and hundreds of workers quickened and fitted for the service of Christ; I point you to literally thousands prayed into the kingdom and I say unto you, "Behold, the purchase of such a price!''

Surely Calvary represents a fearful price. But your soul and mine and the millions thus far redeemed and other millions yet to be redeemed, a wrecked earth restored to Eden perfection, the kingdoms of this world wrested from the grasp of the usurper and delivered to the reign of their rightful King; when we shall see all this, shall we not gladly say, "Behold the purchase!"

One of his dearest friends in India writes about the great change that came in John Hyde's spiritual life at this convention. He writes that though John was a missionary and a child of God, for he had been born of God, he was yet a babe in Christ. He had never been compelled to tarry at his Jerusalem till he was endued with power from on high. But God in His love spoke to him and showed him his great need. At this convention, while he was speaking to his brother missionaries on the work of the Holy Spirit, God spoke to his own soul and opened up to him the divine plan of sanctification by faith. Such a touch of God, such a light from heaven came to him, that he said at the close of the convention: "I must not lose this vision."

And he never did lose it, but rather obtained grace for grace, and the vision brightened as he went obediently forward.

Another missionary tells how John came to this convention to lead the Bible studies. During those days he spoke on the length and breadth and height and depth of the love of God. That mighty love seemed to reach out through him and grip the hearts of men and women and draw them closer to God. This brother writes:

> One night he came into my study about half-past nine and began to talk to me about the value of public testimony. We had an earnest discussion until long after midnight.
>
> We had asked him on the next evening to lead a meeting for men which was being held in the tabernacle out on the compound, while the women of the convention were holding a meeting of their own in the missionary bungalow.
>
> When the time for the meeting arrived the men of us were seated there on the mats in the tent, but Mr. Hyde, the leader, had not arrived. We began to sing, and sang several numbers before he did come in, quite late.
>
> I remember how he sat down on the

mat in front of us, and sat silently for a considerable time after the singing stopped. Then he arose and said to us very quietly, "Brothers, I did not sleep any last night and I have not eaten anything to-day. I have been having a great controversy with God. I feel that He has wanted me to come here and testify to you concerning some things that He has done for me, and I have been arguing with Him that I should not do this. Only this evening a little while ago have I got peace concerning the matter and have I agreed to obey Him, and now I have come to tell you just some things that He has done for me."

After making this brief statement, he told us very quietly and simply some of the desperate conflicts that he had had with sin, and how God had given him victory. I think he did not talk more than fifteen or twenty minutes, then sat down, bowed his head for a few minutes, and said, "Let us have a season of prayer."

I remember how the little company prostrated themselves upon the mats in the Oriental manner, and then how for a long time, man after man rose to his feet to pray, how there was such confession of sin as most of us had never heard

before and such crying out to God for
mercy and help.

It was very late that night when the
little gathering broke up and some of us
know definitely of several lives that were
wholly transformed through the influence
of that meeting.

Evidently that one message opened the
doors of men's hearts for the incoming of
the great revival in the Indian Church.

"Brokenheartedness for Sin"

In the spring of each year the Punjab
Prayer-Union holds its annual meeting. But
as preparation for this meeting the leaders
spend much time in prayers and fastings
and all night watching. Then when the
Union comes together we look to God for
guidance during the coming year.

The next year at that annual meeting
God laid on our hearts the burden of a world
plunged in sin. We were permitted to share
to some extent in the sufferings of Christ.
It was a glorious preparation for the convention in the fall.

At this convention John Hyde was constantly in the prayer room day and night;

he lived there as on the Mount of Transfiguration. The words were burned into his brain as a command from God: *I have set watchmen upon thy walls, O Jerusalem, which shall never hold their peace day nor night: ye that are the Lord's remembrancers take ye no rest and give him no rest till he establish, and till he make Jerusalem a praise in the earth.* (Isa. 62:6, 7).

There can be no doubt that he was sustained by divine strength, for are we not told to endure hardness according to the power of God, not in our own weakness but in His strength?

It was not the quantity but the quality of sweet childlike sleep that our Father gave his servant which enabled him to continue so long watching unto prayer. One could see from his face that it was the presence of Christ Himself that strengthened his weak body. John Hyde was the principal speaker, but it was from communion with God that he derived his power.

He was leader of the morning Bible readings, his subject being John 15:26, 27, "He shall bear witness of me, and ye also shall bear witness of me."

John developed the theme: "Is the Holy

Spirit first in your pulpits, pastors? Do you consciously put Him in front and keep yourselves behind Him, when preaching? Teachers, when you are asked hard questions do you ask His aid as a witness of all Christ's life? He alone was a witness of the incarnation, the miracles, the death and the resurrection of Christ. So He is the only witness!'' It was a heart-searching message, and many were bowed down under the convicting power.

The next morning Mr. Hyde was not allowed to give any further teaching. The chairman came down from his seat and declared the meeting to be in the hands of God's Spirit. How wonderfully He witnessed of Christ and His power to cleanse all who repent! The next morning once again His servant said that he had no fresh message from God. It was pointed out that God would not be mocked—till we had all learned this lesson as to putting the Holy Spirit first at all times, God would not give any fresh message. Who can forget that day? How wonderfully those prayers were answered! The watchmen that night in the prayer room were filled with joy unspeakable and they ushered in the dawn with shouts of triumph. And why not? For we are more than conquerors through Him Who loves us.

At one time John Hyde was told to do something and he went and obeyed, but returned to the prayer room weeping, confessing that he had obeyed God unwillingly. "Pray for me, brethren, that I may do this joyfully."

We soon learned after he went out that he had been led to obey triumphantly. He re-entered the hall with great joy, and as he came before the people, after having obeyed God, he spoke three words in Urdu and three in English, repeating them three times, *"Ai Asmani Bak,"* "O Heavenly Father."

What followed who can describe? It was as if a great ocean came sweeping into that assembly. Hearts were bowed before that Divine Presence as the trees of the wood before a mighty tempest. It was the ocean of God's love being outpoured through one man's obedience. Hearts were broken before it. There were confessions of sins, with tears that were soon changed to joy, and then to shouts of rejoicing. Truly, we were filled with new wine, the new wine of Heaven!

Here is the experience of one missionary:

Hours alone with God, with no one to see or hear but God, were customary; but the fellowship of others in prayer or praise, for hours, could that be real? On entering that room the problem was solved.

At once you knew you were in the holy presence of God, where there could be only Reality. Others in the room were forgotten except when the combined prayers and praises made you realize the strength and power and sympathy of such fellowship. The hours of waiting on God in communion with others were precious times, when together we waited on God to search us and to speak to us, together interceded for others, together praised Him for Himself and for His wonder-working power.

There was breadth and freedom during those ten days that I never imagined existed on earth. Surely it was for freedom such as this that Christ has set us free. Each one did exactly as he or she felt led to do. Some went to bed early, some prayed all night long. Some went to the meetings and some to the prayer room and some to their own rooms. Some prayed, some praised. Some sat to pray, some kneeled, some lay prostrate on their faces before God, just as the Spirit of God bade them.

There was no criticism, no judging of what was being done or said. Each one realized that all superficialities were put away, that each one was in the awful presence of the Holy God.

The same missionary referred to John Hyde when she wrote:

There were some who knew that God had chosen and ordained them to be watchmen. There were some who had lived for long so near Jehovah that they heard His voice and received orders direct from Him about everything, even as to when they were to watch and pray, and when they were to sleep. Some watched all night long for nights, because God told them to do so, and He kept sleep from them that they might have the privilege and honor of watching with Him over the affairs of His kingdom.

The Lamb on His Throne

At the convention the next year, in answer to prayer God poured out on us by His Spirit a burden for lost souls. We saw the same "brokenheartedness" for the sins of others. None felt this more than John Hyde. God was deepening his prayer-life. He was permitted of God to have the privilege of drinking of the Master's cup and of being baptized with His baptism, the second baptism of fire, suffering with Him that we may reign with Him here and now, the life of true Kings for the sake of others.

About this time John Hyde began to have visions of the glorified Christ as a Lamb on his throne—suffering such infinite pain for and with his suffering Body on earth, as it is so often revealed in God's Word. As the Divine Head, He is the nerve center of all the body. He is indeed living today a life of intercession for us.

Prayer for others is as it were the very breath of our Lord's life in heaven. It was becoming increasingly true of John Hyde. How often in the prayer room he would break out into tears over the sins of the world, and especially of God's children! Even then his tears would be changed into shouts of praise according to the divine promise repeated by our Lord on that last night when He talked freely with His own. Ye shall be sorrowful, but your sorrow shall be turned into joy.

There was another example of how this agony of soul in John Hyde was reflected in one who was a daughter in Christ to him. An Indian Christian girl was at this convention. Her father had compelled her to neglect Christ's claims upon her. In the prayer room she was convicted of her sin, and told how her heart was being torn away from her father to Christ. One could almost see the springing tendrils of her heart as the power of the love of Christ came upon her. It was a terrible time.

Then she asked us to pray for her father. We began to pray and suddenly the great burden for that soul was cast upon us, and the room was filled with sobs and cries for one whom most of us had never seen or heard of before. Strong men lay on the ground groaning in agony for that soul. There was not a dry eye in that place until at last God gave us the assurance that prayer had been heard and out of Gethsemane we came into the Pentecostal joy of being able to praise Him that He heard our cry.

A brother writes about that Convention:

Thank God, He has heard our prayers and poured out the Spirit of Grace and intercession upon so many of His children. For example I saw a Punjabi brother convulsed and sobbing as if his heart would break. I went up to him and put my arms about him and said, "The blood of Jesus Christ cleanseth us from all sin."

A smile lit up his face. "Thank God, Sahib," he cried, "but oh, what an awful vision I have had! Thousands of souls in this land of India being carried away by the dark river of sin! They are in hell now. Oh, to snatch them from the fire before it is too late!"

That meeting was one that will never leave my memory. It went on all night. It was a time when God's power was felt as I never had felt it before.

God wants those who are willing to bear the burden of the souls of these millions without God to go with Jesus into Gethsemane. He wants us to do this. It is a blessed experience to feel that in some measure we can enter into the fellowship of Christ's sufferings. It brings us into a precious nearness to the Son of God. And not only this, but it is God's appointed way of bringing the lost sheep back to the fold.

He is saying, 'Who will go for us, and whom shall I send?' Are you who read these words willing to be intercessors? If

we are willing to put ourselves into God's
hands, then God is willing to use us. But
there are two conditions: obedience and
purity. Obedience in everything, even in
the least, surrendering our wills and taking the will of God. And the next step is
purity. God wants pure vessels for His
service, clean channels through which to
pour forth His grace. He wants purity in
the very center of the soul, and unless God
can have a pure vessel, purified by the fire
of the Holy Spirit, He cannot use that vessel. He is asking you now if you will let
Him cleanse away part of your very life.
God must have a vessel He can use!

Holy Laughter

The next summer John went to a friend's
house for a holiday. It was in the hills. The
friend writes about it thus:

The crowning act of God's love to us
personally was the wonderful way in
which he brought Mr. Hyde up to stay
with us. I also had to come up to do duty
among some English troops here. So Hyde
and I have been having glorious times together. There were seasons of great conflict and at times I thought Hyde would
break down completely. But after nights

of prayer and praise he would appear fresh and smiling in the morning.

God has been teaching us wonderful lessons when He calls us to seasons of such wrestling. It is that command in II Timothy 1:8, "Suffer hardship with the gospel according to the power of God." So we have the power of God to draw upon for all our need. Ever since Mr. Hyde realized this he says he has scarcely ever felt tired, though he has had at times little sleep for weeks. No man need ever break down through overstrain in this ministry of intercession.

Another element of power: "The joy of the Lord is your strength." Ah G—, a poor Punjabi brother of low caste origin, has been used of God to teach us all how to make such times of prayer a very heaven upon earth, how to prevent the pleasure of praying and even of wrestling ever descending into a toil. How often has G— after most awful crying seemed to break through the hosts of evil and soar up into the presence of the Father! You could see the smile of God reflected in his face. Then he would laugh aloud in the midst of his prayer.

It was the joy of a son reveling in the delight of his Father's smile. God has been teaching John and me that his name is the God of Isaac—laughter. Have you observed that picture of heaven in Proverbs 8:30? "I was daily in his delight." This is the Father's love being showered upon his own Son. No wonder that in such a home the Son should say that he was "always rejoicing before Him." Rejoicing, laughing, the same word as Isaac. This holy laughter seemed to relieve the tension and give heaven's own refreshment to wrestling spirits.

The Next Summer

The next summer John Hyde again went up to the hills to be with his friends. They later wrote:

His room was a separate one upon the hill, and to one side of our house. Here he came, but came for a very real intercession with his Master. This intercession was fraught with mighty issues for the kingdom of God amongst us.

It was evident to all that he was bowed down with sore travail of soul. He missed many meals, and when I went to his room I would find him lying as in great agony, or walking up and down as if an inward fire were burning in his bones. And so there was, that fire of which our Lord spoke when he said: "I came to cast fire upon the earth, and how would I that it were already kindled! But I have a baptism to be baptized with, and how I am straitened till it be accomplished." John did not fast in the ordinary sense of the word, yet often at that time when I begged him to come for a meal he would look at me and smile and say, "I am not hungry."

No! there was a far greater hunger eating up his very soul, and prayer alone could satisfy that. Before the spiritual hunger the physical disappeared. He had heard our Lord's voice saying to him: "Abide ye here and watch with Me." So he abode there with his Lord, Who gave him the privilege of entering Gethsemane with Himself.

One thought was constantly uppermost in his mind, that our Lord still agonizes for souls. Many times he used to quote from the Old and New Testaments, especially as to the privilege of "filling up that which was lacking of the afflictions of Christ." He would speak of the vow made by our Lord devoting a long drawn out travail of soul till all His own were safely folded. "For I say unto you that I shall not drink henceforth of the fruit of the vine till that day when I drink it new with you in My Father's kingdom." "Saul, Saul, why persecutest thou Me?" These were some of the verses used of God to open his eyes to the fellowship of Christ's sufferings. These were days when the clouds were often pierced and the glorified life that our Lord now leads shone through, revealing many mysteries of travail and pain. It was truly a following of Him who is the Lamb, suffering still with us as He once did for us on earth, though now Himself on the throne. John Hyde found that He still carries our crosses—the heavy end of our crosses, "for He ever liveth to make intercession for us."

It was into the life of prayer and watching and agonizing for others that he was being led step by step. All this time, though he ate little and slept less, he was bright and cheerful.

Our children had ever been a great joy to him. Uncle John, who had so often played with them, was always welcomed with smiles of love. Yet now, even the little ones appeared to realize that this was no time for play! They were wonderfully subdued and quiet in his presence in those days, for there was a light on his face that told of communion with another world.

Yet there was nothing of the hermit about him—in fact people were more than ever attracted to him, and freely asked for his prayers. He always had leisure to speak to them of spiritual things, and entered even more patiently than ever into their trials and disappointments.

We will not speak in detail of those days of watching and praying and fasting when he appeared to enter into our Lord's great yearning for his sheep. We feared his poor weak body would sink under the strain; but how marvelously he was sustained all the time! At times that agony was dumb, at times it was a crying out for the millions perishing before our eyes; yet it was always lit with hope. Hope in the love of God—Hope in the God of Love.

With all that depth of love which he seemed to be sounding with his Lord, there were glimpses of its heights—moments of heaven upon earth, when his soul was flooded with songs of praise, and he would enter into the joy of his Lord. Then he would break into song but they were always Songs in The Night.

In those days he never seemed to lose sight of those thousands in his own district without God and without hope in the world.

How he pleaded for them with sobs—dry, choking sobs, that showed how the depths of his soul were being stirred. "Father, give me these souls or I die!" was the burden of his prayers. His own prayer that he might rather burn out than rust out was already being answered.

Let me introduce here a gem from the pen of Paterson:

What was the secret of that prayer life of John Hyde's? This, that it was a life of prayer. Who is the source of all life? The glorified Jesus. How do I get this life from Him? Just as I receive His righteousness to begin with. I own that I have no righteousness of my own—only filthy rags and I in faith claim His righteousness.

Now, a twofold result follows: as to our Father in heaven, He sees Christ's righteousness, not my unrighteousness. A second result as to ourselves: Christ's righteousness not merely clothes us outwardly, but enters into our very being, by His Spirit, received in faith as with the disciples (see John 20:22) and works out sanctification in us.

Why not the same with our prayer life? Let us remember the word "for." "Christ died for us," and "He ever liveth to make intercession for us," that is, in our room and stead. So I confess my ever-failing prayers (it dare not be called a life), and plead his never-failing intercession. Then it affects our Father, for He looks upon Christ's prayer-life in us, and answers accordingly. So that the answer is far "above all we can ask or think."

Another great result follows: it affects us. Christ's prayer-life enters into us and He prays in us. This is prayer in the Holy Spirit. This is the life more abundant which our Lord gives. Oh, what peace, what comfort! No more working up a life of prayer and failing constantly. Jesus enters the boat and the toiling ceases, and we are at the land where we would be. Now, we need to be still before Him, so as to hear His voice and allow Him to pray in us—nay, allow Him to pour into our souls His overflowing life of intercession, which means literally: face to face meeting with God—real union and communion.

One Soul a Day

It was about this time that John Hyde laid hold of God in a very definite covenant.

This was for one soul a day, not less, not inquirers simply, but a soul saved, ready to confess Christ in public and be baptized in His name. Then the stress and strain was relieved. His heart was filled with the peace of full assurance. All who spoke to him perceived a new life and new life-work which this life can never end.

He returned to his district with this confidence nor was he disappointed. It meant long journeys, nights of watching unto prayer, and fasting, pain and conflict, yet victory always crowned this. What though the dews chilled him by night and the drought exhausted him by day? His sheep were being gathered into the fold and the Good Shepherd was seeing of the travail of His soul and being satisfied. By the end of that year more than four hundred were gathered in.

Was he satisfied? Far from it. How could he possibly be so long as his Lord was not? How could our Lord be satisfied, so long as one single sheep was yet outside His fold? But John Hyde was learning the secret of divine strength: the joy of the Lord. For, after all, the greater our capacity for joy, the greater our capacity for sorrow. Thus it was with the Man of Sorrows, He who could say: "These words have I spoken unto you that my joy may be in you and that your joy may be full."

John Hyde seemed always to be hearing the Good Shepherd's voice saying, "Other sheep I have, other sheep I have." No matter if he won the one a day, or two a day, or four a day, he had an unsatisfied longing, an undying passion for lost souls. Here is a picture given by one of his friends in India:

> As a personal worker he would engage a man in a talk about his salvation. By and by he would have his hands on the man's shoulders, be looking him very earnestly in the eye. Soon he would get the man on his knees, confessing his sins and seeking salvation. Such a one he would baptize in the village, by the roadside, or anywhere.
>
> I once attended one of his conventions for Christians. He would meet his converts as they came in and embrace them in Oriental style, laying his hand first on one shoulder and then on the other. Indeed his embraces were so loving that he got nearly all to give like embraces to Christians, and those, too, of the lowest caste.

This was his strong point. Love won him victories.

Two Souls a Day

Again John Hyde laid hold of God with a definite and importunate request. This time it was for two souls a day. At this convention God used him even more mightily than ever before. God spoke through His servant John Hyde.

We speak with bated breath of the most sacred lesson of all—glimpses that he gave us into the divine heart of Christ broken for our sins. He did not overwhelm us with this sight all at once. He revealed these glimpses gently and lovingly according to our ability to endure it. Ah, who can forget how he showed us His great heart of love pierced by that awful sorrow at the wickedness of the whole world, which grieved Him at His heart.

Deeper and deeper we were allowed to enter into the agony of God's soul, till like the prophet of sorrow, Jeremiah, we heard his anguish, desiring that his eyes might become a fountain of tears, that he might weep day and night for the slain of the daughter of his people. There the divine longing was realized in Gethsemane and Calvary! We were led to see the awful suffering of the Son of God, and the still more awful suffering of the Father and of the Eternal Spirit, through whom He offered up himself without spot unto God.

How can we enter into the fellowship of such sufferings? "Ask, and it shall be given you, seek and ye shall find, knock, and it shall be opened unto you." Observe the progress in intensified desire—great, greater, greatest, and the corresponding reward till, to crown it all, the Father's heart is thrown open to us. Yes, to all and sundry we tell our joys; it is the privileged few very near our hearts to whom we tell our sorrows!

So it is with the love of God. It was to John the beloved as he lay close to the heart of the Master, and then drew closer still, that Jesus revealed the awful anguish that was breaking His heart, that one of them should betray Him. The closer we draw to His heart, the more we shall share His sorrows. All this we obtain only by faith. It is not our broken heart, it is God's we need. It is not our sufferings, it is Christ's we are partakers of. It is not our tears with which we should admonish night and day, it is all Christ's. The fellowship of His sufferings is His free gift for the taking in simple faith, never minding our feelings.

At the end of this convention a dear child of God cried:

> Lord, give me Thy heart of love for sinners, Thy broken heart for their sins, Thy tears with which to admonish night and day,
>
> But, O Lord, I feel so cold! My heart is so hard and dead. I am so lukewarm!

A friend had to interrupt him.

> Why are you looking down at your poor self, brother? Of course your heart is cold and dead. But you have asked for the broken heart of Jesus, His love, His burden for sin, His tears. Is He a liar? Has He not given what you asked for? Then why look away from His heart to your own?

John used to say, "When we keep near to Jesus it is He who draws souls to Himself through us, but He must be lifted up in our lives; that is, we must be crucified with Him. It is self in some shape that comes between us and Him, so self must be dealt with as He was dealt with. Self must be crucified.

"Then indeed Christ is lifted up in our lives, and He cannot fail to attract souls to Himself. All this is the result of a close union and communion, that is fellowship with Him in His sufferings!"

Four Souls a Day

The eight hundred souls gathered in since last year's convention did not satisfy John Hyde. God was enlarging his heart with His love. Once again he laid hold on God with holy desperation. How many weeks it was I do not remember, but he went deeper still with Christ into the shadows of the Garden! Praying took the form now of confessing the sins of others and taking the place of those sinners, as so many of the prophets did in old time. He was bearing the sins of others alone with his Lord and Master. "Bear ye one another's burdens, and so fulfill the law of Christ." According to that law we ought to lay down our lives for the brethren. This John Hyde was doing.

What was that burden referred to in

Galatians 6:2? The previous verse reveals it. It was bearing the sins of others. He at length got the assurance of four souls a day.

Yet this was the year that God used him all over India. He was called to help in revivals and conferences in Calcutta, Bombay, and many of the larger cities. Surely he was being prepared for an eternity-wide mission. Yet he was never more misjudged and misunderstood. But that, too, was part of the fellowship of Christ's pain. "He came unto His own, and His own received Him not."

We who were so privileged saw in John Hyde's life the deepening horror of sin during that year, though it was all but a pale reflection of the awful anguish over sin that at length broke our Saviour's heart.

Before this year's convention he spent long nights in prayer to God. This burden had lain now for five years on his heart, each year pressing heavier and heavier. How it had eaten into his very soul! One saw the long sleepless nights and wary days of watching with prayer written on every feature of his face. Yet his figure was almost transformed as he gave forth God's own words to his people with such fire and such force that many hardly recognized the changed man with the glory of God lighting up every feature. We who had shared some of the burden in prayer knew that it was God's own burden spoken to His Church in India, yes, to His Church throughout the whole world.

The confession of the sins of others laid hold of John Hyde's heart. It was about that time he was taught a very solemn lesson— the sin of fault-finding even in prayer for others. He was once weighed down with the burden of prayer for a certain Indian pastor. So he retired to his inner chamber, and thinking of the pastor's coldness and the consequent deadness of his church, he began to pray: "O Father, thou knowest how cold—"

But a finger seemed to be laid on his lips, so that the word was not uttered and a voice said in his ear, "He that toucheth him, toucheth the apple of Mine eye."

Mr. Hyde cried out in sorrow: "Forgive me, Father, in that I have been an accuser of the brethren before Thee!" He realized that in God's sight he must look at whatsoever things are lovely. Yet he wanted also to look at whatsoever things are true. He was shown that the "true" of this verse are limited to what are both lovely and true, that the sin of God's children is fleeting, it is not the true nature of God's children. For we should see them as they are in Christ Jesus—"complete," what they shall be when He has finished the good work He has begun in them.

Then John asked the Father to show him all that was to be praised ("if there be any virtue and if there be any praise take account of these things") in that pastor's life. He was reminded of much for which he could heartily thank God, and spent his time in praise! This was the way to victory.

The result? He shortly afterwards heard that the pastor had at that very time received a great reviving and was preaching with fire. It is this way of praise which is appointed of God for preparing the Bride and the putting on of her beautiful garments. In Revelation 19:6-8, it is praise that leads to the glorious results.

I remember John telling me that in those days if on any day four souls were not brought into the fold, at night there would be such a weight on his heart that it was positively painful, and he could not eat nor sleep. Then in prayer he would ask his Lord to show him what was the obstacle in him to his blessing. He invariably found that it was the want of praise in his life. This command, which has been repeated in God's Word hundreds of times —surely it is all important! He would then confess his sin, and accept the forgiveness by the Blood. Then he would ask for the spirit of praise as for any other gift of God. So he would exchange his ashes for Christ's garland, his mourning for Christ's oil of joy, his spirit of heaviness for Christ's garment of praise, and as he praised God souls would come to him, and the numbers lacking would be made up.

Soon after the Sialkot Convention, John Hyde held a meeting in Calcutta. His friend in that city writes about him:

> He stayed with us nearly a fortnight, and during the whole time he had fever. Yet he took the meetings regularly, and how God spoke to us through him, though he was bodily unfit to do any work!

> At that time I was unwell for several days. The pain in my chest kept me awake for several nights. It was then that I noticed what Mr. Hyde was doing in his room

opposite. The room where I was being in
darkness, I could see the flash of the elec-
tric light when he got out of bed and turned
it on. I watched him do it at twelve and at
two and at four, and then at five. From
that time the light stayed on till sunrise.
By this I knew that in spite of his night
watches and illness, he began his day at
five.

I shall never forget the lessons I
learned at that time. I had always claimed
exemption from night watches, as I felt
too tired at bedtime. Had I ever prayed
for the privilege of waiting upon God in
the hours of night? No! This led me to
claim that privilege then and there. The
pain which had kept me awake night after
night was turned into joy and praise because of this new ministry which I had
suddenly discovered, of keeping watch in
the night with the Lord's Remembrancers.
At length the pain quite left my chest,
sleep returned, but with it the fear came
upon me lest I should miss my hours of
communion with God.

I prayed, "Lord, wake me when the
hour comes" (see Isa. 50:4). At first it
was at two, and afterwards at four, with
striking regularity. At five every morning
I heard a Mohammedan priest at the
Mosque near by call out for prayers in a

ringing, melodious voice. The thought that I had been up an hour before him filled me with joy.

But Mr. Hyde grew worse, and the annual meeting of his Mission was calling him. Being anxious, I induced him to come with me to a doctor. The next morning the doctor said: "The heart is in an awful condition. I have never come across such a bad case as this. It has been shifted out of its natural position on the left side to a place over on the right side. Through stress and strain it is in such a bad condition that it will require months and months of strictly quiet life to bring it back again to anything like its normal state. What have you been doing with yourself?" Dear Hyde said nothing, he only smiled. But we who knew him and knew the cause: his life of incessant prayer day and night, praying exceedingly with many tears for his converts, for his fellow-laborers, for his friends, and for the church in India!

Then the friend writes how God taught him to live a life of prayer through Mr. Hyde's example, and how afterwards he, too, like John Hyde, was led into the fellowship of Christ's sufferings down, down, down, farther and farther into the very recesses of Gethsemane, till he, too, seemed to treat the winepress of the wrath of God against sin all alone.

Behold how much was wrought in the life and work of one woman missionary. She had worked hard for many years in her district and none of the work there was bearing real fruit. She read the account of Mr. Hyde's prayer-life and resolved to devote the best hours of her time to prayer and waiting on God in the study of His word and will. She would make prayer primary, and not secondary as she had been doing. She would begin to live a prayer-life in God's strength. God had said to her: "Call upon Me, and I will show thee great and mighty things. You have not called upon Me and therefore you do not see these things in your work." She felt that at any cost she must know Him and a prayer-life, and so at last the battle of her heart was ended and she had the victory. One thing she prayed for was that God would keep her hidden. She had to face being misunderstood and being dumb and not opening her mouth in self-defense if she was to be a follower of the Lamb.

In less than a year she wrote a letter,

and oh, what a change! New life every-
where, the wilderness being transformed
into a garden. Fifteen were baptized at
first, and one hundred and twenty-five
adults during the first half of the following
year! So she wrote and continued:

> The most of the year has been a battle
> to keep to my resolution. I have always
> lived so active a life, accustomed to steady
> work all day long, and my new life called
> for much of the best part of the day to be
> spent in prayer and Bible study. Can you
> not imagine what it was, and what it is
> sometimes now? To hear others going
> around hard at work while I stay quietly
> in my room, as it were inactive.
>
> Many a time I have longed to be out
> again in active work among the people in
> the rush of life, but God would not let me
> go. His hand held me with as real a grip
> as any human hand and I knew that I
> could not go. Only the other day I felt
> this again and God seemed to say to me,
> "What fruit had ye in those things whereof
> ye are now ashamed?"
>
> Yes, I knew I was ashamed of the years
> of almost prayerless missionary life.
>
> Every department of the work now is
> in a more prosperous condition than I have

ever known it to be. The stress and the
strain have gone out of my life. The joy
of feeling that my life is evenly balanced,
the life of communion on the one hand and
the life of work on the other, brings con-
stant rest and peace. I could not go back
to the old life, and God grant that it may
always be impossible.

Another year passed, and she wrote
again:

The spirit of earnest inquiry is in-
creasing in the villages and there is every
promise of a greater movement in the fu-
ture than we have ever had. Our Chris-
tians now number six hundred in contrast
with one sixth of that number two years
ago. I believe we may expect soon to see
great things in India. Praise for His hourly
presence and fellowship!

When I was a boy there was a pond near
my father's house. I would stand on the
shore of that pond and throw a stone out
into the water and then watch the waves
in ever-widening circles move out from that
center, till every part of the surface of the
pond would be in motion. The waves would
come to the shore at my very feet and every
little channel and inlet would be moved by
the ripples.

Sialkot started circles and waves of blessing that are even now beating in the secret recesses and inlets of many human hearts. Only God and the recording angel can determine how much the whole body of Christ has been moved upon and benefited by the tremendous prayer force generated by the Holy Spirit in that prayer room at Sialkot.

Native pastors, teachers and evangelists have gone home from these conventions with new zeal for Jesus Christ and have influenced thousands of lives in their many fields of labor.

Foreign missionaries have had their lives deepened by visions of God. Letters and printed pages, like the aprons and handkerchiefs from Paul's body, have been sent probably to every country on earth to bring healing to the faint-hearted, and direction and encouragement to those desiring to enter the prayer life.

I am assured that tens of thousands have been born into the kingdom because of the soul travail at Sialkot. Myriads will one day rise up to thank God that two or three men in North India in the name of Jehovah said, "Let us have a convention at Sialkot!"

England Again

The next spring, John Hyde started home a very ill man. He had arrived in India in the autumn of 1892, less than twenty years before. But surely they were nineteen beautiful years!

When he arrived in England, he went to visit some friends in Wales, intending later to attend the Keswick Convention. While in Wales he heard that Dr. J. Wilbur Chapman and Mr. Charles M. Alexander, on their worldwide evangelistic tour, were holding a meeting at Shrewsbury. With two of his friends he went to the opening of this campaign. During the first stay of three days a friend writes: "We greatly enjoyed the services, but we realized that there was some great hindrance and this was felt especially at the meeting for ministers."

"After that service we saw that the burden had come upon Mr. Hyde, and as we were leaving the next day he asked whether we could engage his room at the hotel for the following week. He was preaching on the Sunday at another place; but he intended returning early Monday morning to take up the burden of prayer for Shrewsbury. To those who knew him, it was apparent that the load was weighing very heavily upon him. The faraway gaze, the remarkably sweet, pathetic, pained expression, the loss of appetite, the sleepless nights, all went to prove this."

Later Dr. J. Wilbur Chapman was to write:

God has been graciously near to us in all these long journeys around the world, and we have learned some things which have increased our faith.

First, more than ever before, we believe in the Bible as the authentic Word of God.

Second, we believe in prayer as never before. I have learned some great lessons concerning prayer. I know that all great revivals are born of prayer.

At one of our missions in England the audience was extremely small, results seemed impossible but I received a note saying that an American missionary was coming to the town and was going to pray God's blessing upon our work. He was known as "Praying Hyde."

Almost instantly the tide turned. The hall was packed, and my first invitation meant fifty men for Jesus Christ. As we were leaving I said, "Mr. Hyde, I want

you to pray for me." He came to my room,
turned the key in the door, dropped on his
knees, waited five minutes without a single syllable coming from his lips. I could
hear my own heart thumping and beating.
I felt the hot tears running down my face.
I knew I was with God. Then with up-
turned face, down which the tears were
streaming, he said: "Oh, God!"

Then for five minutes at least, he was
still again, and then when he knew he was
talking with God his arm went around my
shoulder and there came up from the
depth of his heart such petitions for men
as I had never heard before. I rose from
my knees to know what real prayer was.
We believe that prayer is mighty, and we
believe it as we never did before.

Mr. Charles M. Alexander related further particulars about this meeting. Not only did Dr. Chapman meet John Hyde, but
Mr. Alexander was present also. And the
three of them spent almost the whole day
in conference about the meeting. Then the
other workers were called in, and a long
time was spent in prayer. After that the
Spirit was present in the meetings in such
power that all barriers were broken down
and sinners were crying for mercy and

being saved all over the house. Mr. Hyde
had a helper in intercession in the person
of Mr. Davis of the Pocket Testament
League, and the two, being kindred spirits,
became very friendly.

Mr. Hyde remained there for a whole
week and then went back to his friends in
Wales. The following day he was seriously
ill and could scarcely speak, but he smiled
and whispered: "The burden of Shewsbury
was very heavy, but my Saviour's burden
took Him down to the grave."

The manner in which John Hyde prayed
as described by Dr. Chapman, that is, paus-
ing between petitions, is also referred to
by another writer:

Right on his face on the ground is Praying Hyde. This was his favorite attitude for
prayer. Listen! he is praying; he utters a
petition, and then waits; in a little time he
repeats it, and then waits; and this many
times until we feel that that petition has
penetrated every fibre of our being and we
feel assured that God has heard and without doubt He will answer. How well I remember him praying that we might open
our mouth wide that He might fill it (Ps.
81:10). I think he repeated the word

'wide' scores of times with long pauses
between. "Wide, Lord, wide, open wide,
wide." How effectual it was to hear him
address God, "O Father, Father!"

A lady who was for years a missionary
in India wrote:

I remember, during one of the Jubble-
port Conventions at the noon-tide prayer
meeting, I was kneeling near to him, and
can never forget how I was thrilled with a
feeling I cannot describe as he pleaded in
prayer: "Jesus — Jesus — Jesus!" It
seemed as if a baptism of love and power
came over me, and my soul was humbled
in the dust.

Home at Last

"And the toils of the road will seem nothing,
When we come to the end of the way."

When John Hyde arrived in New York,
he went at once to Clifton Spring, N.Y. His
purpose was to obtain relief from a severe
headache from which he had suffered much
before leaving India. An operation revealed
a malignant tumor, diagnosed as sarcoma.
He rallied from this operation, and in Sep-
tember went to his sister, the wife of Prof.
E. H. Mensel, at Northampton, Mass.

But soon after New Year's he began to have pains in his back and side. He thought it was rheumatism, but the physician knew it was the dreaded sarcoma again.

John Hyde passed away February 17, 1912. His body was taken by his brother Will and his sister Mary back to the old home at Carthage, Illinois, and the funeral was held in the church where his father was for seventeen years the pastor. The Rev. J. F. Young, John's classmate, was pastor of the home church and preached at the funeral. It was my privilege to assist in the service and to stand on the platform and look down into the casket at that dear, dear face. He was greatly emaciated but it was the same sweet, gentle yet strong, resolute face that I had known in 1901, the last time I saw him alive.

That February the 20th was cloudy and chill and gloomy, as out in beautiful Moss Ridge we tenderly laid him beside his father and his mother and his brother Edmund. But I know that by and by the clouds and the shadows will flee away, the chill and gloom of the grave be dispelled, and that man of prayer and praise come forth in the likeness of the Risen Son of God!

Holiness Unto the Lord

As I have carefully and prayerfully gone over the facts and incidents and experiences in the life of my dear friend, I am impressed that the one great characteristic of John Hyde was holiness. I do not mention prayerfulness now, for prayer was his life-work. I do not especially call attention to soul-winning, for his power as a soul-winner was due to his Christ-likeness.

God says, "Without holiness no man shall see the Lord," and we may scripturally say without holiness no man shall be a great soul-winner. Mr. Hyde himself said in substance, "Self must not only be dead but buried out of sight, for the stench of the unburied self-life will frighten souls away from Jesus."

It does not seem that John Hyde preached much about his own personal experience of sanctification, but he lived the sanctified life. His life preached. Just as he did not say very much about prayer, he prayed. His life was a witness to the power of Jesus' Blood to cleanse from all sin.

Not only was his the word of a prophet,

but his life had been sanctified by the truth. One day a missionary was talking to a young Hindu who had become acquainted with Mr. Hyde, when the Hindu said: "Do you know, Sir, that Mr. Hyde seems to me like God." He was not far from the truth, for in a sense unknown to his Hindu understanding this man had become an incarnation. I quote from a postal card written by John to his sister while he was at Clifton Springs, N.Y., "Am still in bed or wheel chair, getting a fine rest and doing a lot of the ministry of intercession, and having not a few opportunities of personal work."

How the radiance of holiness shone out in Jesus' every word and deed! Yes, dear heart, and we can truthfully and reverently say, How the radiance of holiness shone out in John Hyde's every word and deed.

A cry of anguish and a song of praise!